Grocers

by Alison Behnke

Lerner Publications Company • Minneapolis

Text copyright © 2006 by Lerner Publications Company

Lerner Publications Company
A division of Lerner Publishing Group
241 First Avenue North
Minneapolis, MN 55401 U.S.A.

Website address: www.lernerbooks.com

Words in **bold type** are explained in a glossary on page 31.

Library of Congress Cataloging-in-Publication Data

Behnke, Alison.
        Grocers / Alison Behnke.
            p.   cm. – (Pull ahead books)
        Includes index.
        ISBN-13: 978-0-8225-2801-2 (lib. bdg. : alk. paper)
        ISBN-10: 0-8225-2801-0 (lib. bdg. : alk. paper)
        1. Grocers—Juvenile literature. I. Title. II. Series.
    HD8039.G8B44 2006
    381'.456413–dc22   2005004325

Manufactured in the United States of America
1 2 3 4 5 6 – JR – 11 10 09 08 07 06

Uh oh! The refrigerator looks kind of bare. Who can help?

The grocer!

The grocer works at a shop
that sells food.

The grocer sells groceries to many people in your **community**.

Your community is made up of people in your neighborhood, town, or city.

Some grocers own small shops.

Others work in large grocery stores called **supermarkets**.

Grocers sell many kinds of food. They sell everything from fruit to ice cream. They sell vegetables and breadsticks and salad dressing.

Where do grocers get all of this food?

Most grocers
buy food from
people called
wholesalers.

Wholesalers buy very large amounts of food from farmers and factories. Then they sell smaller amounts to grocers.

Grocers pick out the food that they want to order. They buy things that they think their **customers** will like.

Customers are people who buy foods and other things from the grocer.

The wholesaler
delivers the food
to the grocer.
Usually it comes
in a big truck.

The grocer makes sure that the food is fresh and clean before he puts it out in the store.

The grocer also makes sure that the store looks nice and neat. She tries to make customers want to shop there.

The grocer keeps track of what foods
are most popular. That is how she
knows what people want to buy.

Most grocers hire people to help them run their stores. **Stockers** help put the food on the shelves.

Cashiers add up the cost of the food. They take money from customers and give them change.

In some grocery stores, **baggers** put the groceries in bags. They might also carry them out to your car.

When you get
to the grocery
store, all of
these people
are ready to
help you!

Any questions? The grocer can answer them.

He will help you find what you're
looking for. He can tell you about
different foods.

Grocers make sure that their customers are happy and get what they need.

Thanks to the grocer, you can go home and fill up the refrigerator!

Facts about Grocers

- Many grocers sell more than just food. They might sell flowers, magazines, or household things such as soap and paper towels.

- Some grocers work at stores called co-ops. A co-op is set up by a group of people in the community. These people all own the store together. They all get to help decide what it sells and how it works.

- Supermarkets are common in the United States. But in many other countries, only big cities have supermarkets. In smaller towns, grocers work in small stores and sell only certain foods. A grocer who sells only fresh fruit and vegetables is called a greengrocer. A person who sells meat is called a butcher. Bakers sell bread, and fishmongers sell fish and seafood.

- Grocers care about making their stores look nice. They may set up special displays for holidays or to focus on certain foods.

Grocers through History

People have always needed food, so grocers have been important for a long time. But the kinds of places where people buy food have changed over the years. So have the ways that grocers help people.

■ Shoppers used to give grocers lists of everything they wanted to buy. Grocers went and got all the foods and brought them back to the customers.

■ The first self-service grocery store, where customers got the foods themselves, was called Piggly Wiggly. It opened in Memphis, Tennessee, in 1916.

■ Big supermarkets are common now. But they haven't always been around. King Kullen is famous for being the first supermarket. A grocer named Michael J. Cullen opened King Kullen on Long Island, New York, in 1930.

More about Grocers

Check out these books and websites to find out more about grocers. Or visit a local shop and see if you can talk to the grocer there.

Books

dePaola, Tomie. *Tom.* New York: Putnam's, 1993.

Krull, Kathleen. *Supermarket.* New York: Holiday House, 2001.

Pluckrose, Henry. *In the Supermarket.* New York: Franklin Watts, 1998.

Schaefer, Lola M. *Supermarket.* Chicago: Heinemann Library, 2000.

Websites

National Grocers Association
http://www.nationalgrocers.org

USDA for Kids
http://www.usda.gov/news/usdakids

Glossary

baggers: workers who put groceries in bags at the grocery store

cashiers: workers who add up the cost of everything that a customer buys. Cashiers also take money or other payment from customers.

community: a group of people who live in the same city, town, or neighborhood. Communities share the same fire departments, schools, libraries and other helpful places.

customers: people who buy something from a shop or store

stockers: workers who put food out on the shelves in a grocery store

supermarkets: large stores that sell groceries and other things

wholesalers: people who buy large amounts of food and sell smaller amounts to grocers

Index

The photographs in this book appear courtesy of:

© Sam Lund/Independent Picture Service, pp. 3, 4, 5, 6, 8, 11, 12, 13, 14, 16, 17, 18, 19, 20, 21, 23, 24, 26, 27; © Todd Strand/Independent Picture Service, pp. 7, 22; U.S. Department of Agriculture, pp. 9, 25, 29; © Nana Twumasi/Independent Picture Service, p. 10; © Beth Johnson/Independent Picture Service, p. 15.

Front Cover: Sam Lund/Independent Picture Service.

Special thanks to the Wedge Co-op and employees.